AT THE GREAT DOOR OF MORNING

Also by Robert Hedin

POETRY

The Light under the Door
Poems Prose Poems
The Old Liberators: New and Selected Poems and Translations
Tornadoes
County O
At the Home-Altar
Snow Country

TRANSLATIONS

The Lure-Maker from Posio: Prose Poems of Dag T. Straumsvåg (with Louis Jenkins)
The Dream We Carry: Selected and Last Poems of Olav H. Hauge (with Robert Bly)
A Bumpy Ride to the Slaughterhouse: Prose Poems of Dag T. Straumsvåg
    (with Louis Jenkins)
The Roads Have Come to an End Now: Selected and Last Poems of Rolf Jacobsen
    (with Robert Bly and Roger Greenwald)
The Bullfinch Rising from the Cherry Tree: Poems of Olav H. Hauge
The Dream Factory: A Children's Story by Bjørn Sortland (with Emily Christianson)
Night Music: Poems of Rolf Jacobsen

EDITED COLLECTIONS

Where One Voice Ends Another Begins: 150 Years of Minnesota Poetry
Old Glory: American War Poems from the Revolutionary War to the War on Terrorism
Perfect in Their Art: Poems on Boxing from Homer to Ali (with Michael Waters)
Keys to the Interior: Twenty-Five Years of the Great River Review (with Richard Broderick)
The Zeppelin Reader: Stories, Poems, and Songs from the Age of Airships
The Great Machines: Poems and Songs of the American Railroad
The Great Land: Reflections on Alaska (with Gary Holthaus)
Alaska: Reflections on Land and Spirit (with Gary Holthaus)
In the Dreamlight: Twenty-One Alaskan Writers (with David Stark)

ROBERT HEDIN

At the Great Door of Morning

Selected Poems and Translations

WITH A FOREWORD BY TED KOOSER

COPPER CANYON PRESS

Port Townsend, Washington

Cover art: Mel Ziegler, *An American Conversation: Sandhills far,* 2013, Seneca, Nebraska. This image documents a four-hour lightning event that took place in conjunction and in conversation with a local rancher.

Copper Canyon Press is in residence at Fort Worden State Park in Port Townsend, Washington, under the auspices of Centrum. Centrum is a gathering place for artists and creative thinkers from around the world, students of all ages and backgrounds, and audiences seeking extraordinary cultural enrichment.

LIBRARY OF CONGRESS CATALOGING-IN-PUBLICATION DATA

Names: Hedin, Robert, 1949– author.
Title: At the great door of morning : selected poems and translations /
    Robert Hedin.
Description: Port Townsend, WA : Copper Canyon Press, [2017]
Identifiers: LCCN 2016043706 (print) | LCCN 2016052942 (ebook) | ISBN
    9781556595042 (softcover) | ISBN 9781619321687 (E-book)
Subjects: | BISAC: POETRY / American / General.
Classification: LCC PS3558.E318 A6 2017 (print) | LCC PS3558.E318 (ebook) |
    DDC 811/.54—dc23
LC record available at https://lccn.loc.gov/2016043706

9 8 7 6 5 4 3 2 FIRST PRINTING

COPPER CANYON PRESS
Post Office Box 271
Port Townsend, Washington 98368

www.coppercanyonpress.org

for Carolyn
for Alex, Ben, and Katie
for Selma

CONTENTS

TRANSLATIONS

Selected Translations of Rolf Jacobsen

Selected Translations of Olav H. Hauge

Selected Translations of Dag T. Straumsvåg

SELECTED POEMS, PART 2

A novelist friend once told me he thought *The Great Gatsby* was a perfect work in that it made not a single misstep. It seems to me that *At the Great Door of Morning* is another perfect work, each of its poems and translations expertly tuned and thoughtfully presented to its strongest, most moving effect.

I have been reading Robert Hedin's fine poems and translations for many years, and I have yet to find anything faulty about any of them. (I might have said, "about the least of them," though I would be hard put to find a "least" among them.) I've met Robert, and from what I've seen, everything about the life he leads seems to be in perfect order, appears to have been the very best choice of what to do. So it is no wonder that he would not let a single poem go out into the world until it was ready.

I am not talking about competency. There are thousands of competent poets in our country. This poet has moved beyond competency as though it had been a middle-school phase of his artistic development. His work has moved on into meaningfulness, into beauty, into art.

Dana Gioia was once asked by a young professor what his "project" as a poet was, and he replied, "My project is to break your heart." And that's what I'm looking for in reading a poem, to be that deeply moved. I want more than anecdote, more than cleverness, more than erudition. I want what Jim Harrison described as poems with "human heat." And thanks to Robert Hedin and Copper Canyon Press, here they are, a whole book of them.

We live in a narcissistic society, quite possibly the most self-absorbed society ever, as evidenced by millions of daily Facebook postings. And surely others besides me have guiltily enjoyed reading in the news of someone taking a "selfie" at the Grand Canyon and falling back over the edge. Thus it is a great pleasure to read poems in which the "I" is either absent or is present as a clear-sighted, unsentimental witness. The speaker in these poems never shows us despair and self-pity; here are awe and wonder. Here's Hedin, in the "Field Notes" section of this book: "A good poem breaks through the numbing, stultifying voice of our mass culture to successfully articulate, in all its breadth and meaning, a landscape of conviction, a deeper circuitry that helps give life its necessary shape and substance."

In addition to Hedin's own poetry, three Norwegian poets are here translated to good effect. That is, the resulting works, in American English, are poems in their own right, and the identity of the translator is veiled or hidden. I am reminded of the opening of the popular BBC series *Downton Abbey,* where we see the hands of, one presumes, the butler, using a ruler as he checks to see whether the table setting has been done to his satisfaction. The art of translation is much like that, consisting as it does of carefully arranging words, like china, silver, and glassware on a table, while wearing gloves. Hedin has made the arrangement and has left few fingerprints.

In these pages you'll find your own poems to love. I especially enjoy the tornado poems, which mirror the way in which weather anecdotes are delivered in everyday speech. I've studied the reminiscences of people who've survived weather disasters, and these poems by Hedin have that kind of authenticity. However, the poems I return to again and again are those in which Hedin is out walking the world and telling us what he is seeing, such as those poems set in Europe. He is for me the perfect guide, his job to direct our attention to things we should notice. If an "I" appears, it is only in the service of authenticity.

Fifteen thousand years ago, when the human family was living at the mouths of caves, one of us would venture deep into the forest looking for something to eat and would then come back to tell the rest what he or she came upon out there. It was the account of that experience that most mattered to us, not the teller who had survived it. We wanted a good telling, and still do. Here is Robert Hedin at the edge of the firelight, offering us the wonders he has seen.

Ted Kooser

AT THE GREAT DOOR OF MORNING

Selected Poems, Part 1

Moving Out with the Finches

for Sherod Santos

This morning I'm going to drag my desk
Out into the backyard and set it down
By the birdbath, near the flower bed
Overgrown with weeds. And the black
Leather armchair where I like to read
I'll lug out under the two young maples,
Along with the Persian rug, the tall
Goosenecked lamp, the books, the CDs,
Even the huge unruly fern in the corner.
I'm going to haul it all outside, out
Into the open air where it's quiet,
Where I won't be bothered,
Out by the lilacs, the trellis of roses,
Near the blossoming fruit trees
Where they like to gather, the finches,
Those little birds, the color of pollen.

My Mother's Hats

She kept them high on the top shelf,
In boxes big as drums—

Bright, crescent-shaped boats
With little fishnets dangling down—

And wore them with her best dress
To teas, coffee parties, department stores.

What a lovely catch, my father used to say,
Watching her sail off into the afternoon waters.

Raising the *Titanic*

I spent the winter my father died down in the basement,
under the calm surface of the floorboards, hundreds

of little plastic parts spread out like debris
on the table. And for months while the snow fell

and my father sat in the big chair by the Philco dying,
I worked my way up deck by deck, story by story,

from steerage to first class, until at last it was done,
stacks, deck chairs, all the delicate rigging.

And there it loomed, a blazing city of the dead.
Then painted the gaping hole at the waterline

and placed my father at the railings, my mother
in a lifeboat pulling away from the wreckage.

Bells

for M.L., killed in Vietnam

I remember it was 1965, the summer
    I was put in charge
        of the bells. Above me
and high up, they waited
    like thunderheads at the top
        of the First Presbyterian Church.
And so each Sunday I would pull,
    and down out of that dark
        ringing would fall,
like flecks of glittering mica,
    dead moths, flies, and the small
        luminous bones of bats.
But most of all it was dust.
    And all summer with the sun
        high in its arc,
and the heat building slowly
    by degrees, I rose, lifted
        by that long bell rope,
and, swinging there, would pull
    the dust down, like light,
        over the bowed, sleeping Bibles.

Rowing Lessons

Today I'm out on the river,
    teaching my boys
        how to plant

and pull, to work
    the oars deep, what
        my father taught me,

the simple mechanics
    of it all: how each oar
        is a wing, each

stroke a beat. Then
    pass them to my sons,
        and off we go,

gliding, both boys
    side by side, shoulder
        to shoulder.

And so it goes on, oar
    and oarlock, this keeping
        the river moving.

The Old Swede

Strange, how I think of him every time
I take a bath: down in that little room

Off the cellar stairs, sprawled out
Full length in the long, white hull

Of the tub, belting out the hymns
They brought over from the old country,

The ones he used to sing in steerage.
Some nights even now I hear him

All over the house, every room,
His big voice booming through the vents.

The Greatest

for Michael Waters

What I remember most about Muhammad Ali
Are not the fast hands and loose, graceful footwork.
Or Manila or Zaire. Or even what came after—
The slurred speech, the sad slow shuffle.
No, what I remember is a boy somewhere
In the foothills of the snowy Zagros Mountains,
A small Kurdish boy in a long blue robe
Who gave us directions that day we were lost,
And how he knew nothing of America
But two syllables he sang over and over
In the high-pitched voice of a girl—
Ali, Ali—then laughed and all at once
Began to bob and weave, jabbing and juking,
His robe flaring a moment like a fighter's.
Ali. One word, two bright syllables
That turned to smoke in the morning air.
And he pointed down the long, dusty road
To Hatra and Ur, the ruins of Babylon,
And the two ancient rivers we had read about,
Their dark starless waters draining away into fog.

Mincielli

Everyone agreed Mincielli wasn't the same after the big roan reared up and kicked him broadside in the head. Not many could survive a blow like that, and he spent the next week blacked out, a bump big as a walnut over his right ear. For sure he wasn't dead, but he wasn't of this world either. We just figured he was lost somewhere in between and hoped he'd find his way back. When he finally came to, he wasn't the same old Mincielli anymore. He was friendlier, more agreeable. It was as though he'd been away on vacation, and just sat in the bakery telling everyone where he'd been, how balmy the weather was there, and how glad he was to be home now, back at his job in the feedstore, all rested and ready for work.

How Drabowski Became Famous

The last time I saw Drabowski was the afternoon of the big
hailstorm. I was out in the yard checking for damage when
he came by, his body all bruised, battered, his left foot drag-
ging behind the right like a piece of luggage. And when I
called out to see how he was doing, he threw up a hand
and said he was fine, "a little sore maybe, but just fine," and
kept on going, past the dented pickup, the smashed glass,
the power lines crackling like lightning, hobbling off into
the late afternoon to join the rest of the wreckage.

Miss Sanvidge

What happened to my old trumpet with the three sticky valves and mouthpiece all battered beyond shining? Or for that matter those long hours I spent languishing away in the last chair of the high-school band room, stumbling through Sousa, "Taps," "The Star-Spangled Banner." And what happened I wonder to Miss Sanvidge and her dusky parlor where we used to sit side by side that summer I took up the piano, her little plaster bust of Beethoven scowling down as I plugged away week after week—beautiful, middle-aged Miss Sanvidge, who every Tuesday set the metronome ticking.

Basic Math

Seventy-two beats per minute, 4,320 an hour. That's 103,680 a day, or 37,843,200 a year. Now subtract for the cigarettes, the bourbon, the sleepless nights, the lost weekend in the Poconos. That leaves 567,600,000 taps until the clouds part, the dust bows down, until the little black train comes to take me away, O Lord. All this I calculated this morning, Ash Wednesday, as I sit here under duress—one hand over my heart pledging allegiance, the other drumming furiously at the calculator, while snow drifts down over the empty lawn chairs, the flakes too many to count—and dedicate to Pythagoras, Euclid, and all the other early mathematicians, but mostly to those three overworked draft horses who darkened the stables at Washington Elementary—Miss Keeley, Miss Ramsey, and Miss Loper—whom I thank now for the flash cards, the mountains of homework, and the long-suffering hours I spent at the blackboard, adding columns taller than I was. May they rest in peace, wherever they are.

My Mother Turns Ninety

I should mention that all this time
It's been getting darker, the light
So poor I can barely see my breath,

How everything now is tired
Of climbing, even the smoke rising
In great strides over the rooftops
Wants to lie down at rest with the rain.

An Hour Ago

In the small dusty
Galaxy of the garden,

Where the hydrangeas
Are all bright blue

And bask like planets
In the morning light,

I could hear Bashō
Hard at work, hoeing.

The Bank at Fourth & Main

Even Audubon would like this place,
This aviary of young, colorful birds.

All day they glide from desk to desk,
From one dusty perch to another,

Chirping away to the sweet music
Of money, the whole flock waiting

For five when they migrate back
To their roosts in the suburbs,

The bright wings of their shawls
Filling the drafty flyway of the street.

Out Pruning

In the garden this morning,
I thought for a moment
I saw T'ao Ch'ien.

But it was just one
Of my old hydrangeas
Swaying in the cool breeze,
Nodding its great dusty head.

Turning Sixty

So this is how it must've looked,
The gates to the garden
Creaking shut,
And both of them
Standing there in late-afternoon light,
Looking back, the rain pelting
Down hard, the flowers
Closing their shutters,
The leaves already beginning to fall.

Not the Way They Used to Make Love

Standing up, fumbling over clasps
And hooks, boxers and pink panties

Puddled at the ankles. Or sprawled out,
Spread-eagled, those wild furtive nights

On the Persian rug, the kitchen table,
Bra dangling from the dusty galaxy

Of the chandelier. But only now,
If at all, in the dusky bedroom, rocking

Side by side in the last slant of sunlight,
Their tired, broken-down bodies

Rising once more to the old familiar task
Of making each other beautiful again.

The Afterlife of Airships

Here the *R101* still lounges
At its mooring mast,

And the *Akron* and *Macon*
Lie side by side in the shade,

Their great dusty hulls
Overgrown with weeds.

And the *Hindenburg*
Is not all smoke and ash,

But floats peacefully,
Barn swallows wheeling

Through its shadow,
Its huge ghostly outline

Basking like some prize
Melon in the morning sun.

The Great Liners

The age of the great liners is over now.
Titanic, Britannic: they lie
On the bottom like broken cathedrals.

But imagine how beautiful they were:
Gleaming star lobes, chandeliers,
Staircases winding into blinding light.
Five, six stories tall, they loomed
Before us like bright cities.

Andrea Doria, Lusitania:
On the last day they will rise
And take their place in the night sky.
The dead will peer from their staterooms
Into the stellar dark,
And we who call ourselves survivors
Will stare into the vast
Stories of light,
The earth made buoyant by their passing.

Fliers

Lindbergh, Dornier, Lilienthal...
I pronounced each one
and listened
as they rose in formation off my tongue.

Myron

The first time it happened he was up on his roof shingling. The second time he was stringing Christmas lights along the eaves. The neighbors saw a shadow pass the kitchen window, then heard a thump like a sack of potatoes hitting hard. Pretty soon it happened so many times people lost count. They'd hear the familiar thump and knew Myron had just tumbled off his roof again. No one could figure him out. How stupid can you get, they said. When he wasn't falling, Myron was hobbling around town, sporting a fresh cast, some new fracture, his body so broken up no one thought he could make the climb. But there he was, right on schedule, every Saturday hauling the big ladder out from his garage and hoisting the rungs into the sunlight, where he liked to go.

Rain

One morning all over town it began to rain, little down-
pours breaking out in the bakery, the laundromat. By nine
it was thundering in the beauty parlor, drizzling in the jew-
elry store. All morning it kept pelting down, big plump
drops cascading over tables, countertops, wreaking havoc in
the hardware store, in the barbershop splattering on what-
ever heads it could find. There was no reason for the rain,
no logical explanation. Then someone recalled the people
who'd lived here first. How they'd prayed for rain, how their
gods lived high in the mountains miles away and some-
times wouldn't answer for years, old senile gods who often
became confused, how perhaps they were the ones who'd
sent the rain, the little thunderheads massed at the ceilings.

Houses at the Arctic Circle

All winter long they float in the cold, little fleets of wood and tar paper. Then one day the mercury climbs, the permafrost thaws, and there's water everywhere, water seeping through the floorboards, pouring in by the gallon. It's almost like going down at sea. One minute you're lying in bed, snug and warm with your cargo of houseplants, your ballast of books; the next you're gurgling like a carp on the bottom. Who says life is fair? At nine the next morning the mailman comes to the gate. No house, no dog. All he finds is a leaky oil drum bobbing on the surface. That's the third one this week, he says to himself, then turns and trudges off. All summer it goes on like this, houses bubbling down into the gloom, whole villages disappearing from maps, plat books. And the mailmen? They're like some lost tribe, out there wandering the vast emptiness, pouches bulging with news, unpaid bills.

Afterward

Afterward everything hung in perfect balance. Light and dark, heaven and hell. We weighed our words carefully and never went outside. We just wandered the house, one desolate room after another, afraid anything we'd say, even the slightest comment, would bring the day crashing to the floor. And so finally we settled on no words at all, and lost ourselves in little things—watering the plants, straightening the books on the bookshelves—both of us wondering how long it could last. It was like some great scale, so fragile, so delicately calibrated, even the dust was a factor, could tip the day one way or the other.

Family Reunion

The first to arrive was the boy in blue pants, then the young man in the white sailor suit. They came early, in the dark, and stood side by side in their little mantles of light on the lawn. And later, after the sun rose, others arrived. They came unannounced, uninvited, and lined up under the shade trees, not saying a word, not even a hello. Then, one by one, starting with the boy in blue pants, they began telling their stories— long, sad stories that went on hour after hour. By the time they were done it was early evening, and their shadows had overwhelmed the lawn. And the man who'd waited all day, the one standing so long at the gate, listening, thought at last it was his turn, and he started in from the little pool of the yard light.

The Wreck of the Great Northern

Where the Great Northern plunged in
The river boiled with light, and we all stood
In the tall grass staring at a tangle
Of track, and four orange coaches
And one Pullman lying under the current,
Turning the current clear. We stood staring
As though it had been there all along
And was suddenly thrust up out of the weeds
That night as a blessing, as a long, sleek hallway
Dropping off into fields we'd never seen,
Into the pastures of some great god
Who sent back our steers too heavy to move,
All bloated and with green seaweed strung down
Their horns. And we all looked down
Into the lit cars at businessmen
And wives, already back to breathing water,
And saw in the cold, clear tanks of the Pullman
A small child the size of my son, a porter's
White jacket, a nylon floating gracefully
As an eel.
                        What the train and the river
Were saying, no one could understand.
We just stood there, breathing what was left
Of the night. How still the cars were,
How sleek, shimmering through the undertow.
And I saw the trees around us blossomed out,
The wind had come back and was blowing
Through the tall empty grass, through the high
Grain fields, the wind was rattling
The dry husks of corn.

Houdini

There is a river under this poem.
It flows blue and icy
And carries these lines down the page.
Somewhere beneath its surface
Lying chained to the silt
Harry holds his breath
And slowly files
His fingernails into moons.
He wonders who still waits at the dock
If the breasts of those young girls
Have developed since he sank.
He thinks of his parents
Of listening to the tumblers
Of his mother's womb
Of escaping upward out of puberty
Out of the pupils in his father's eyes
And those hot Wisconsin fields.
He dreams of escaping
From this poem
Of cracking the combinations
To his own body
And those warm young safes
Of every girl on the dock.
Jiggling his chains
Harry scares a carp that circles
And nibbles at his feet.
He feels the blue rush of the current
Sweeping across his body
Stripping his chains of their rust
Until each link softens
And glows like a tiny eel.

And Harry decides to ascend.
He slips with the water
Through his chains
And climbing over and over
His own air bubbles
He waves to the fish
To his chains glittering
And squirming in the silt.
He pauses to pick a bouquet
Of seaweed for the young girls
On the dock. Rising
He bursts the surface of this poem.
He listens for shouts.
He hears only the night
And a buoy sloshing in the blue.

Sloughing

Back here in the bottomlands
The sloughs lie flat
As hides, breathing quietly
Among dead trees
And reeds. It's June,
Almost fifteen years
Since we stripped
And waded into these warm
Lungs, drifting among turtles
And sunfish, in what was dying
Or dead, or having to grow
Simple to survive.
You stood knee-deep
In the smoke off the water,
Naked and wet with algae,
The old rotted shell
You'd found lifted up
Into the cold light
Like a horn, a white strand
Of fish eggs dripping
From your neck like seeds.

Tanner's Creek

All I know is what I was told:
Swim there and you die.
There was down
By the local landfill
Where the tanners dumped their sludge.
Glowing, nearly iridescent,
It bubbled, even belched,
And once I remember
Overflowed,
Roiling in our flowers
And flower beds,
And not even frogs would go near.
And the tanners—
On summer nights they'd gather
Under the floodlights
In the parking lot,
Or back behind the old abandoned spur,
Smoking and talking low
In the shadows
Of the empty cattle cars,
Big coarse men
In long leather aprons
And gloves
That swallowed half the arm.

Rattlesnake Bluff

That night the lack of rain brought them
Down off the bluff,
All we saw was the grass
Fluttering where we'd burned,
And occasionally in the hot flashes
Of light, a long body stretched out off the porch
Shimmering in the dew. The next morning
When we found the hens dead
In the yard, the froth
On the cow's udder,
The skin wrapped like jewelry
Around the cold jars of preserves,
You loaded the gun and we climbed halfway up
The huge slope, leading each other around
Until we found one
As thick as our wrists,
So sluggish it could only dive once
And miss. When you pulled
And its head flew off like a bottle cap,
What little water the earth had given up
Was only good for cooling
Our hands, for wiping
The long blade after the rattles were loose.

Pollen

For weeks it was our weather,
Clouding the air for days,
A fine bright storm that billowed
Over barns and feedlots,
Making all the livestock shine,
The horses one color.
And like luck I wanted it to last,
To have it there each morning
When I milked, the stalls
And stanchions shining,
The udders all dusted with light.

Rowboats

Always a surprise to see them,
Out here on the farm belt,

Miles from any water, hulls
Riddled and gone to dry rot

In the tall weeds beside barns
And dusty fleets of outbuildings.

You see their keels flashing
In the late-afternoon light

As you drive by on your way
To Plainview, Bellechester,

A great many boats,
Enough to make a small navy.

The Old Swede's Feet

How they had carried him everywhere,
Across dance floors, parade grounds,
The Pacific. And every day for forty years

To work and back. How I could hear them
In the early mornings, down in the cold
Ungodly dark, padding the worn tile,

The blank linoleum. How they creaked
And popped, and never saw the light
Of the sun. What he called his dogs,

And would dangle every Saturday night
Over the long, white gunwales
Of the tub. And never complained,

Never said a word, just sat there
After supper in his dim pool of smoke
And lamplight, kneading them

Over and over like bread dough,
Working his way down until each bone,
Each starved splinter gave up its grief.

The Old Scandinavians

You should hear the old Scandinavians
Singing in their white clapboard churches—
The Danes and buttoned-down Norwegians,
The tall, big-boned Swedes with shocks
Of white hair. You should hear them
Hoisting their voices from this world
To the next. I mean those bachelor farmers
Sitting in the back pews, the ones
Bellowing away in their starched collars
And same gray suits every Sunday,
Those old Carusos from Bergen, Trondheim,
The last ones left from the big crossing.
You should hear them rejoicing in their little
Drafty churches with the one-story steeples,
Under the bells that haven't rung in years.

Hunting Agates at White Rock

All day alone and stripped to the waist,
The sweat gleaming on the hairs
Of my stomach. Two miles
South in the gravel pit
At White Rock, and there's nothing
But my own breath going out
Among these stones. Where is the tooth
My grandfather unearthed here,
The mastodon molar as big and brown
As his old gnarled fist? Or the rock
I heaved at the harmless bull snake,
And the light burning that day
Off the stones? As a boy
I used to go silent for days,
Trying to hear how the earth sounds
To the dead, and heard the huge
Silver tumbler in the cellar
Grinding the stones day and night
Until they came out gray
With sludge and needed washing
Under the hose. Now there is nothing
But the earth at White Rock
Lying open like a grave,
With just enough light to gather
My stones. Soon the winds will come,
And the first martins flying
For the night into the bottomlands,
The heat lightning a mile out
Over the floodplain.
And the long walk up County O,
Following those three stars

That come full circle to bless
The thornbush I darkened with blood,
And the old Baptist cemetery
Where the Swedes of White Rock
Lay down in the winter of '39,
My grandfather among them,
And found home in these stones.

Translations

On Translation

When translating, I work in two linguistic landscapes at once, and much of my time is spent trying to reconcile the conflicting demands of both. It is not always a pleasant task, never an easy one, and it often requires a great deal of patience, deference, and a willingness to compromise.

In many ways, I act as a mediator in a constant tug-of-war, with each language trying to dominate the other. Invariably, certain sacrifices have to be made, and each language must surrender some of its territory.

The challenges that one encounters—linguistic, aesthetic, cultural, and historical—are not only inevitable but often unsolvable. The most one can do is to honor the spirit of the original by fitting the language into its larger, aesthetic dimensions. The result is something that closely mirrors the original, more refraction than reflection, more re-creation than reproduction.

Ultimately, all translations must survive on their own merits and possess the necessary critical elements that draw us to poetry in the first place. Like others who translate, I work with the understanding that none of my efforts is definitive and that no translation can ever equal the original.

My task is to render the inner life of the poem without losing sight of the humbling, rather unnerving fact that I am articulating the intimate and powerful tool of another human's voice in all its varied fullness.

Selected Translations of Rolf Jacobsen

When They Sleep

All people are children when they sleep.
There's no war in them then.
They open their hands and breathe
in that quiet rhythm heaven has given them.

They pucker their lips like small children
and open their hands halfway,
soldiers and statesmen, servants and masters.
The stars stand guard
and a haze veils the sky,
a few hours when no one will do anybody harm.

If only we could speak to one another then
when our hearts are half-open flowers.
Words like golden bees
would drift in.
God, teach me the language of sleep.

Moss, Rust, and Moths

Moss rises from the ground.
Quiet as bats at night,
it settles on the stones and waits,
or down in the grass
with ashen wings.

Rust passes from bolt to bolt,
from iron slab to iron slab in the dark,
and closely examines
if the time is right.
When the pistons have come to rest,
when the girders have gone deep into the night,
it will do its quiet, bloody work.

The stars like white moths
cluster at the dark windowpanes of heaven
and stare
and stare at the city lights.

Night Music

The constellations will change,
the Big Dipper's handle
will be pulled to the south
and Orion lose his sword
before the last pain is gone,
says the stone.

I too
am allotted my share.
As the fountain's glittering dust
springs up and falls back into itself,
all my days come from somewhere inside me,
doled out in a bowl of stone.

There's a calm light around old trees.
They let the wind flow through their leaves,
and stars pass high over their crowns
in majestic procession.

The Fly in the Telescope

It happened that a fly got into the telescope,
like a thorn in eternity's eye
one night when Sirius was high overhead,

and dazzled the astronomer to tears
when he saw the dark hole in the heavens
like a fist of nothing
driven through nothing.

Where is the arm that can hold me fast
and the power that can free my soul from death
—Oh, Mr. Cembalo, come here, will you,
something has happened to the universe! —

Until the fly saw fit to relieve itself
in the constellation of the Swan,
between the wild sun Deneb
and the shimmering flecks of Cepheus
that can only be seen in great telescopes.
Deo Gloria.

Are They Waiting for a Star?

The clouds float back and forth through the wind's doors
with their eternal linens in their arms.
They spread the sheets and shake the quilts,
and prepare the deep silky beds
in every room on earth.

Are they waiting for a star, or for the Old Moon
or a new Almighty God
to finally lie down here at rest
so all will be right with the world.

They're always busy, shaking out their fresh linens,
the earth's housekeepers, waiting for guests
who never come.

Dies illae

The sky's great swarm of stars will circle your feet like jewels, Lord,
and the mountains lie before you as thresholds,
that day when all things are released from their laws,
when the birds are merely a song, and the waterfall a white light
and forest and ocean and sleep are one thing: deep music.
That day when those birds of passage—human hearts—
return to their forgotten May.

What will you say to me then, God Zebaot:
Be a lump of clay on the road,
or be a flower in my forest?

The Buses Long to Go Home

The buses long to go home.
They wait here in line at the terminal and long to go home
to Lualalambo, Nkongsamba, and to Calabar,
and to the flamingo's cry at dusk.

For when it rains in the streets
it rains too in Lualalambo, Nkongsamba, and in Calabar,
not on umbrellas but on
the long-legged stork, and on the female hippos
under the pepper trees.

When they come waddling through the flooded streets,
plastered with wet mud,
they are happy, but it has to be
a tepid rain, cool and gurgling
down the windows with reflections
of Lualalambo, Nkongsamba, and of Calabar,
and female hippos sleeping under pepper trees.

The Morning Paper

The morning paper unfolds on the 7:35 commuter
and suddenly all the men have white wings.
They fly off in space inside the coach
with strange stiff faces
—a procession behind glass
as if to an exclusive private funeral on a star.

The Art of Flying

One great whoosh and we part from the earth oh no
everything rises at a slant like the decks of a ship,
down sail our childhood the gateway summer crushes
swept into a drawer to be saved for the next book of Moses.

Oh, we are wind and clouds and goodbye to Bjordammen,
far below Sinbad the Sailor and Odysseus,
Columbus, Amundsen with his frozen whiskers
drives his sled dogs across the polar ice,
you light a cigarette over the fields of Bethlehem.
Put it out over Calvary it doesn't matter,
the stewardess comes smiling with a new pack.

Fasten your seat belts Signori—a city down there
comes sailing up in the dark like an ocean liner,
with parties on every deck and the faint
red glow of a thousand restaurants,
but what should we do with the blue-black sky, now silent—
the weariness in the backs of our minds and the emptiness
        between the stars
—We came here so suddenly and suddenly
we are alone.

Antenna-Forest

Up on the city's roofs are great plains.
The silence crawled there when no room was left for it on the streets.
Now the forest follows.
It has to be where the silence lives.
Tree after tree in strange groves.
They can barely manage since the floor is too hard.
It's a sparse forest, one branch to the east
and one to the west. Until they resemble crosses. A forest
of crosses. And the wind asks:
Who rests here
in these deep graves?

But We Live—

—But we live
through supermarkets and racks full of cheese, and we live
under vapor trails of jets in the golden month of May
and in smoke-dimmed cities,
and we live with coughing carburetors and slamming car doors.
We live
through the TV-evening in our golden century,
on asphalt, behind tabloids and at gas stations.
We live
as statistics and as registration numbers in election years.
We live with a flower in the window,
in spite of everything we live under
hydrogen bombs the threat
of nuclear extermination, sleep-
less we live
side by side with the hungry who
die by the millions, live
with a weariness to our thoughts, live
still, live
magically inexplicably live
on a star.

Breathing Exercise

If you go out far enough
you'll see the sun as just a spark
in a dying fire
if you go out far enough.

If you go out far enough
you'll see the whole wheel of the Milky Way
rolling away on the roads of the night
if you go out far enough.

If you go out far enough
you'll see the universe itself,
billions of light-years, all of time
as just a glimmer, as lonely and distant
as a star on a June night.

And yet, my friend, if you go out far enough
you'll just be at the beginning

of yourself.

Look—

The moon thumbs through the book of the night.
Finds a lake on which nothing's printed.
Draws a straight line. That's all
it can do.
That's enough.
A thick line. Straight to you.
—Look.

Just Delicate Needles

It's so delicate, the light.
And there's so little of it. The dark
is huge.
Just delicate needles, the light,
in an endless night.
And it has such a long way to go
through such desolate space.

So let's be gentle with it.
Cherish it.
So it will come again in the morning.
We hope.

Selected Translations of Olav H. Hauge

Slowly the Truth Dawns

To wake, and know
your heart sinks
dark and heavy,
hardening into stone...

Slowly the sea lifts its waves,
slowly the trees turn red in the gorge,
slowly the fires begin to lap in hell,
slowly the truth dawns...

The Everyday

The great storms
are behind you now.
Back then you never asked
why you were or
where you came from, where you were going,
you were simply a part of the storm,
the fire.
But it's possible to live
in the everyday as well,
the quiet gray day,
to plant potatoes, rake leaves,
or haul brush.
There's so much to think about here in this world,
one life's not enough.
After work you can roast pork
and read Chinese poetry.
Old Laertes cleared brambles
and hoed around his fig trees,
and let the heroes battle it out at Troy.

We Don't Sail the Same Sea

We don't sail the same sea,
though it looks the same.
Rough-cut timber and iron on deck,
sand and cement in the hold,
I ride low, plunge
headlong through breakers,
wail in fog.
You sail in a paper boat,
your dream fills its blue sail,
so soft the wind, so gentle the wake.

It's the Dream

It's the dream we carry
that something wondrous will happen,
that it must happen—
that time will open
that hearts will open
that doors will open
that the mountain will open
that springs will gush forth—
that the dream itself will open,
that one fine morning we'll drift
into a harbor we didn't know was there.

Erratic Boulder

What an extraordinary place
to settle on,
on a ledge, poised
on the brink.
Don't you value your own success?

One Word

One word
—one stone
in a cold river.
One more stone—
I'll need many stones
if I'm going to cross over.

What do you think?

OUR MISSION:

Poetry is vital to language and living. Copper Canyon Press publishes extraordinary poetry from around the world to engage the imaginations and intellects of readers.

Thank you for your thoughts!

BOOK TITLE: _____

COMMENTS: _____

_____

_____

Can we quote you? ☐ yes ☐ no

☐ Please send me a catalog full of poems and email news on forthcoming titles, readings, and poetry events.

☐ Please send me information on becoming a patron of Copper Canyon Press.

NAME: _____

ADDRESS: _____

CITY: _____ STATE: _____ ZIP: _____

EMAIL: _____

 Copper Canyon Press
A nonprofit publisher dedicated to poetry

MAIL THIS CARD, SHARE YOUR COMMENTS ON FACEBOOK OR TWITTER, OR EMAIL POETRY@COPPERCANYONPRESS.ORG

CopperCanyonPress.org

BUSINESS REPLY MAIL

FIRST-CLASS MAIL   PERMIT NO. 43   PORT TOWNSEND WA

POSTAGE WILL BE PAID BY ADDRESSEE

Copper Canyon Press
PO Box 271
Port Townsend, WA 98368-9931

NO POSTAGE
NECESSARY
IF MAILED
IN THE
UNITED STATES

Poem

If you can make a poem
a farmer finds useful,
you should be happy.
A blacksmith you can never figure out.
The worst to please is a carpenter.

The Old Poet Tries His Hand at Being a Modernist

He too wanted to try
these new stilts.
He's gotten himself up,
and strides carefully like a stork.
Strange, how farsighted he is.
He can even count his neighbor's sheep.

I Have Three Poems

I have three poems,
he said.
Who counts poems?
Emily tossed hers
in a trunk, I
doubt if she counted them,
she simply opened another tea bag
and wrote a new one.
That was right. A good poem
should smell of tea.
Or of raw earth and freshly cut wood.

Today I Knew

Today I knew
I'd made a good poem.
The birds chirped in the garden when I stepped out,
and the sun stood bright over the Berga hills.

Today I Saw

Today I saw
two moons,
one new
and one old.
I have a lot of faith in the new moon.
But it's probably just the old.

Green Apples

Summer was cold and rainy.
The apples are green and flecked with scurf.
But I pick and sort
and stack crates in the cellar.
Green apples are better than nothing.
This farm lies latitude 61° north.

T'ao Ch'ien

If T'ao Ch'ien
comes to visit someday, I will
show him my cherry and apple trees.
I hope he'll come in the spring
when they're all in bloom. Then we'll relax in the shade
over a glass of cider, perhaps I'll show him
a poem—if I can find one he'd like.
The dragons that pass across the sky trailing smoke and poison
flew quieter in his day, and more birds sang.
There's nothing here he wouldn't understand.
More than anything he'd want to get away
to a small garden like mine.
But I'm not sure his conscience would let him.

Anxiety

There's nervous energy in everything now: anxiety in the sunlight,
anxiety in the stars, the earth, anxiety
in the grass, the hornets' nest, tension
in men and women, friction
in cars, planes, and wires,
a charge in the stove,
the coffeepot,
the cat—
jolt, jolt, jolt,
there's current
in everything one touches,
Olai claims.
That's why he stands in rubber boots,
digging himself down
to the blue clay, the cold water.

The Last Spider

Above Sveig, so
      high in the peaks
           the heather was about

to give up, I came upon
      the last
           spider, she

had caught herself
      in her own web.

Summer had been
      cold, few
           mosquitoes, few
                if any moths,

and the flies had
      stayed down where
           things were fatter.

Yes, I just happened on
      this ragged juniper
           where a spiderweb

hung, trembling,
      in the autumn wind.

I See You've Learned

I like
how you
use
few words,
few words and
short sentences
that drift
in a fine rain
down the page
with light and air
between.
I see you've learned
to make
a woodpile in the forest,
good to stack it
tall
so it can dry;
build one long and low
and the wood just sits there and rots.

One Poem a Day

I'll write one poem a day,
every day.
That should be easy enough.
Browning did it for a while, though
he rhymed and
beat time
with his bushy eyebrows.
So, one poem a day.
Something strikes you,
something occurs,
something catches your eye.
—I get up. It's lighter.
Have good intentions.
And see the bullfinch rise from the cherry tree,
stealing buds.

The Old Poet Has Made a Line

The old poet has made a line.
And he's happy, happy as a cider bottle
in spring after it's sent
a fresh bubble up
and is about to pop its cork.

In the Parker Pen

In the Parker pen are many poems, a whole kilometer,
and in the inkwell even more,
mile after mile. Papers
arrive in the mail, bills, advertisements, forms
to be filled out.
I go confidently into the future.

I Aim a Little Higher

For an arrow to strike, it can't make
much of an arc. Still, a good hunter
allows for wind and distance.
So when I aim at you, I aim a little higher.

I Have Lived Here

I have lived here more than a generation.
Years with wind and stars in the high rigging
have sailed by.
Trees and birds have settled in,
but I have not.

From the War

A bullet skittered to rest on the hall floor.
I weighed it in my hand.
It had gone through glass and
two timbered walls.
I had no doubt it could kill.

New Tablecloth

A new yellow cloth on the table.
And new white pages!
Here the words will surely come,
here to such fine cloth,
such fine paper!
The ice rested on the fjord,
and the birds drifted down to settle.

Not by Car, Not by Plane

Not by car,
not by plane—
by neither hay sled
nor rickety cart
—or even by Elijah's fiery chariot!

You'll never get farther than Bashō.
He got there by foot.

When All Is Said and Done

Year in, year out, you've bent over books.
You've gathered more knowledge
than you'd need for nine lives.
When all is said and done,
so little is needed, and that much
the heart has always known.
In Egypt the god of knowledge
had the head of an ape.

I Stop under a Lamppost on a Snowy Evening

for Ernst Orvil on his eightieth birthday

There, at last, I see
    the solitary lamppost
        at the crossroads

holding its umbrella
    of light steady
        in the snowy evening.

I stop, though I have
    no love letter
        begging

to be read. It just
    seems strange
        to pause here

under this lamp
    in such heavy snow,
        and watch the flakes

float awhile
    through the bright
        halo of light

before they swirl back
    into the dark or
        drift quietly down.

And around me in the night
    it keeps on snowing.

Snow in Castile

In Castile they welcome the snow the same way
we greet the fruit blossoms in spring.
That's why Machado sings so beautifully of snow,
snow on Castile's sunbaked rusty hills!
A shadow sleeps beneath the snow on the olive branches.
I think of my orchards at home,
bitten so often by frost.

I Pass the Arctic Circle

A man on the train points out the cairn on the mountain.
We're passing the Arctic Circle, he says.
At first we don't see any difference,
to the north the land looks the same,
but we know where we're headed.
I wouldn't have noticed this little event
if I hadn't, one of these days, passed seventy.

The Carpet

Weave me a carpet, Bodil.
Weave it with visions and dreams,
weave it out of wind,
so I, like a Bedouin, can
roll it out when I pray,
wrap it around me
when I sleep,
and every morning call out:
The table is set!
Weave it as
a cape
against the cold,
as a sail
for my boat!
One day I'll sit down on the carpet,
and sail away
to another world.

Selected Translations of Dag T. Straumsvåg

Cartoon Trick

A man walks upside down through town. Eyes, nostrils, sus-
penders. Everything is upside down. It's completely differ-
ent from a man walking on his hands. Today has been hell,
he says, which means today has been heaven. His head is
level with our toes, and it's difficult to keep up a decent con-
versation. Back pains, collisions with lampposts, photogra-
phers, TV preachers. "This will put our town on the map,"
the mayor thinks. "Maps are good," his wife says.

The Map

Finally, I've decided to make the long-awaited trip to town. I'm out of most things: proteins, iron, carbohydrates, expectations. I'm going to buy that old map I've been looking at. It's a detailed map of my favorite place by the river, a checked cloth heaped with food and drinks. The girl I love lounges at the water's edge. She turns and says, "I wish this could last forever." But the map is a forgery, nothing is right. Not a single landmark is where it should be. And the compass points are all wrong. Not even the people are right, dressed as they are for a different life, miles from the river.

Remedy

When I was young, exorcisms were quite common, a remedy not unlike ice baths. Plus, devils were shorter in those days just as people were. They hadn't eaten enough fruits or vegetables, and lacked essential vitamins and iron, grew thin and pale, fell easily into brooding depressions. They looked more like deer than sheep, and when they possessed you it was usually because they were fleeing from someone else and didn't realize where they were until it was too late. It was more a question of giving directions than driving them out. "Turn right at the hairdresser's, go straight until you get to the abandoned schoolhouse, then turn left. You should see the exit from there." "Thank you. I was completely lost." "You're welcome. Good luck." "You too, and thanks again."

The Campgrounds

Turning right instead of left. It's easy. A small mistake, a rash moment, and you end up some place completely different than you ever imagined. Here at the campgrounds I no longer know where I am. Everything looks the same. Sausages and pork chops. Men and women. "We're all one big family!" And they're friendly, pointing in every direction. Badminton instead of war. The grass keeps coughing up shuttlecocks all through September.

Late at night. Everyone asleep in their tents. Fishermen and farmers under the strict regime of the canvas. All magic is forbidden. The list of *Don'ts* goes on longer than the summer here.

Dr. Alfred

He came down with this disease, a small disease, but it was all he had. His parents were dead, his friends gone. At first he was reserved. Then he noticed the disease had social skills that he lacked himself. People opened up when they visited, talked more. He cared for the disease with a loving hand, carried it with him wherever he went. He watched it grow into a strain no one had ever seen before, and he blossomed at the attention they got. Then the disease grew stronger, took more and more control. It participated in TV debates, went out on the town alone. "Only specialists will be there. You wouldn't understand a thing." Late one night the disease told him they had to talk. "I'm sorry to have to tell you this, but you and I have grown apart. I'm moving in with Dr. Alfred. You remember Alfred? We've been seeing each other secretly for several months. We're *so* good together."

Karl

The police telephoned again today. "We're sorry, Karl, but he got away this time, too. You better lock your doors and stay inside until further notice." This is the fifth time the officer has called, and it's always the same message for a man named Karl. Each time I want to tell him he's got the wrong number, that I'm not Karl, I don't know any Karl, but I end up holding my tongue. It feels so safe to be updated this way, to know the police care enough to look after you. But then, of course, there's Karl. I don't trust him. There's something elusive about the man. Actually, no one has heard from him since all this began.

The Prose Poem

I like to think of the prose poem as an explorer setting sail for the open sea, lost in the legends of El Dorado or Soria Moria, the dream of a new world where everything is possible, anything can happen. But it's hard to tell whether such places really exist; they don't appear on any maps. After a few months, the sailors are all homesick and stricken with scurvy, a sinking feeling they have wasted their lives. It's more likely then the prose poem is a case of vodka hidden away in the engine room of the *Titanic,* used as a card table by the machinists after a long, hard watch, all of them hungry for action, for something unexpected to happen— sudden riches, some excitement at least, a drink while counting their losses.

Debts

We owe Thomas and Elizabeth dinner. We owe my grand-mother a visit to her grave. We owe my brother Christ-mas presents for the last two years, and Lars a solid win at bridge. We've neglected our garden for years, to say noth-ing of Mrs. Hansen next door. We owe our cat more sand, the IRS $22,000, and the wife's boss a beating from long ago. We owe the changing weather several weeks of flu. Over the garden fence, the yellow rubber duck has capsized, its legs sticking straight up in the air. We owe it a resurrection. And now, down the block, the mailman comes with a heap of new bills. We owe him so much. We'll never be able to pay him what he deserves.

Appraisal in Autumn

We sit in the park, and we're not happy. Cold wind, no
money, and God only knows what else is hanging by a
thread over our heads. The prognosis for winter is gloomy.
We asked for too much: the moon and stars instead of bread
and milk, the best gun. Life is quite simple, a question of
hit or miss. Moonlight seeps through a hole in the clouds.
We go in circles like carousel horses at the amusement park.
Back in the casino, Grandmother is working the slots, try-
ing to beat her despair.

Out of Breath

I'm always a little late for the goings-on in my life. This is why I've never landed a decent job, never had a full meal. I'm just not around when the big decisions are made. I arrive when it's all over, out of breath and a little peevish, just in time to see the bus pull away from the depot. If I had a car, I'd follow it out of town to make sure you didn't get off, that I wasn't the one waiting for you, stop after stop, with nothing to offer, nothing to say.

November

It happens so fast. One night you're lying in bed staring out the window at the moon, the dark, at nothing—and suddenly a blood vessel bursts in the brain, a car swerves off the road. It's not you, but someone close to you. You're stunned by the informality of it all. Sometimes the important things collapse so fast, so irreparably, they get seared into your memory. But soon things fade, and you forget. For one reason or another, they're not as important as you thought. You have other worries now. High blood pressure, too little time, your wife driving up from Oslo on slippery asphalt. You know you're in for a long, hard night. You won't take your eyes off the road for a second.

In a Hotel in Riga

Late one night the phone rings, but no one is there, no one on either end. It's as if conversations broken off years ago have suddenly started up again on their own, or those that went to the wrong numbers have finally figured out where they went wrong and now make the right phones ring. But no one answers, and the conversations are sucked back into the lines, colliding, getting mixed up with incoherent discussions, disastrous misunderstandings. This time it's for me, but I'm spending the night at a different hotel, sleeping like a log on a water bed. Down in the depths a goldfish noses around in the dream sludge, and on the wall, blinking neon lights up the faceless portraits of retired civil servants.

Two Rooms and a Kitchen

The previous tenant could write with both hands simultaneously, the landlord says, shaking his head. Two rooms and a kitchen. A bath. On the hat rack a pair of gloves. One of them, the one I believe belonged to his left hand, looks remarkably like the other.

The Fisherman

Unlike other poets, I have only imaginary readers. They're a strange, unruly crowd. All they can agree on is the quality of my poems. They arrange readings and annual conventions, praising my "extraordinary ability to raise failure to a new level." I'm imaginary, too, a tall dark man with a voice that can make women faint, the invention of an unemployed fisherman on a pier, counting gulls until the next Social Security check comes in.

Urho Sariainen

"Do you like fishing?" I ask Urho Sariainen, the fabled eighty-year-old lure-maker from Posio who has honored our town this summer with a visit. A pioneer in the field, he began working with traumatized lures in the early '70s— lures with rusty hooks in their mouths, fins all torn off, gills slashed, eyes reflecting advanced paranoia and depression, faces frozen in fear only encounters with death can cause. "Fishing's no picnic," the old master says, scratching a one-eyed Rapala on its belly.

Poster Poem

It's one of those glossy posters with a motif of the Rocky Mountains which kids like to hang up in their rooms. A green lake, hillsides in clear autumn colors, high snow-capped peaks. At the near end of the lake there's a log cabin. Two men appear on the front steps, stretching and yawning in the chill morning air. "I could get used to this," Harold says, "fishing in the lake, hiking in the mountains." "I'm not sure," Frank whispers, "but I think we're being watched."

The Codfish

Despite what marine biologists say, the codfish is not all that ravenous or tough. It doesn't devour *everything* that comes in its path, and it doesn't like desolate waters any more than the next fish. For thousands of years it's patrolled the seams between warm and cold ocean currents, and rather recently showed the Europeans the way to America. The trouble is, the codfish can't remember a thing. It might swim to Labrador or Lofoten for twenty straight years and not recall any of it. On good days its memory lasts maybe three seconds. Say, is that a herring or a lure? When mistaken, it won't put up a fight; it won't even try to slip off the hook. It's had enough and throws in the towel. Life's just not fair. Or is it? The codfish really can't remember.

Postcard with Elephants

The reason elephants live to be so old is because they breathe slowly and explore each breath thoroughly. Given their ability to store memories for a depressingly long time, they have no problem analyzing the information they gather. It's a scientific project. The elephants' basic theory is that all living creatures have an allotted number of breaths to live on. When a herd passes the corpse of a young elephant, they examine it long and systematically, and always arrive at the same conclusion: fast breathing. It's a plague. Elephants have no respect for athletes. Way too much puffing and panting. They'd mention it to someone, but they have their own problems. The mating season always demands enormous amounts of breath. All that fighting and trumpeting. So they take long walks and try to think up more rational breathing techniques, but this only excites them more, and they end up breathing faster than ever. It's a terrible problem, and they're not even close to solving it. They sigh heavily and lumber on, farther and farther into the dry savanna, deep in thought.

Resurgam in the Delta Pavonis System

Most inventions are inspired by things in nature. Think of the wheel. Or the computer. The computer is not unlike the human brain, complex and frail, a bearer of bad tidings: "A fatal error has been detected in Station C." Station C is the base camp for a group of archaeologists. For three years they have been looking for signs of intelligent life in the Mantell Sector, North Nekhebet, Resurgam in the Delta Pavonis system. A cold and relentless wind blows across the dry plains. The only things the three-day hurricane didn't destroy were an iron shovel and the ship's log. I'koor, the last survivor from Station C, writes: "This expedition has been a failure from day one. There wasn't any sign of intelligent life out here until we arrived, and now I'm going to hit myself over the head with this shovel."

UFOs in the Norwegian Countryside

Unlike in the US, UFOs in Norway don't often land in the countryside. Instead we have domestic flying saucers, especially at Christmastime. With no warning, they fall out of the clear, blue sky, crashing in our blond hair, making mystical patterns in our brain waves. What do they want? Are they hostile? We don't have a clue. Even our wives shake their heads, unable to speak. There's a high-pitched humming sound, as if the computer inside is still working, as if someone had survived and is speaking frantically in a strange tongue, someone who has all the answers to our questions. We believe the scientific approach works best, so we secure the crash site, inspect and catalogue each piece of wreckage. The temperature is quickly falling below zero. We gather around the fireplace, a bewildered bunch of primates picking lice out of each other's hair in the faint December light.

A Quiet Week

It's been a quiet week in the cave, and the Neanderthal fingers a hairball he found in the stomach of a musk ox. A greasy hairball, and he realizes he can mold it into any shape he wants, whatever his hands are capable of making. He pats the hairball into a cube, makes pellets out of tallow, then smears them in random patterns on every side. Beautiful. There's something modern, almost minimalist, about the form. It's perfect for our times, he thinks, simple and clear. But is it practical? He lobs it into the air, balances it on his head, rolls it across the cave floor. He can hardly take his eyes off it. What pattern will show up when it stops? He throws it one more time and tries to guess. After five attempts, he gets it right. He exhales, stands up, walks over to the cave door. This is something completely new. "Does this mean we'll have to climb one more rung on the evolutionary ladder?" his wife sighs. "These are turbulent times," he says. "Anything can happen."

About the Poets

ROLF JACOBSEN was born in 1907 and lived much of his adult life in Hamar, a town north of Oslo, Norway, where he worked as a journalist and newspaper editor. Widely recognized as one of the great Scandinavian poets of the twentieth century, he published numerous volumes of poetry and played a critical role in the introduction of modernism to Norwegian poetry. Rolf Jacobsen died in 1994.

OLAV H. HAUGE is among Norway's most distinguished poets of the twentieth century. During a writing career that spanned nearly fifty years, he produced seven books of poetry, five collections of translations of French, German, and English literature, and five volumes of diaries. A largely self-educated man, he was born in 1908 and earned his living as a farmer, orchardist, and gardener on a small plot of land near his birthplace of Ulvik, a village in the Hardangerfjord region of western Norway. Olav H. Hauge died in 1994.

DAG T. STRAUMSVÅG was born in 1964 in Kristiansund, a city on the sparsely populated coastline of western Norway, and raised in the nearby village of Tingvoll. He has been employed as a farmhand, sawmill worker, librarian, and sound engineer for a radio station in Trondheim, where he has lived since 1984. The author of three books of poetry, Straumsvåg is a respected translator of contemporary American poetry and serves as founding editor and publisher of Pir forlag, an independent book publisher specializing in poetry.

Selected Poems, Part 2

Moving from One Century to Another

First, the constellations have to be taken down. Then the pulleys and cogwheels, the gear work that makes them turn. All dismantled, boxed up, and lugged across the threshold. Then put back again. The galaxies unraveled. The planets dusted, polished, and set spinning on their hubs. And all the racks and pinions, bevels and spurs, recalibrated, reoiled, and started up again, wheeling over the rooftops. Sun and moon, the tiny millstones of the stars.

Fence Wire

Fathers in the 19th century were all called *Papa,*
Could always be seen dragging things
Back from the woods.
                        The wind was a millstone,
And the weather nothing if not dust.
And sometimes all day
They'd stand out
Under the sun, the heat hard as a fist,
Stringing fence wire.
                        And like the pain
Of the century, it gleamed
And was fine-tuned,
It's what the fathers kept
Casting out, tightening, till it sang like fish line.

On Tuesdays They Open the Local Pool to the Stroke Victims

for my sons

Thank God my own father didn't have to go through this.
Or I'd be driving him here every Tuesday
So he could swim his laps
Or splash around with the others
In the shallow end. Something terrible
Has been bled out of these lives. Why else
Would they be here pulling themselves along on their sides,
Scissoring, having to prove to their middle-aged sons
They can still dance.
                  The last three days I heard water
In the cellar, the rooms below me bumping together
Like dinghies. Somewhere back in my sleep
My father splashes in the shallow end.
All these men, even
The balding ones waiting behind the chain-link fence
Watching their fathers, are down there
At the bottom of the stairs.
They are all gliding like sunlight,
Like trout across the cold floors of their breeding ponds.

Tornado

Four farms over it looked like a braid of black hemp
I could pull and make the whole sky ring.
And I remember there falling to earth that night
The broken slats of a barn, baling wire, straw and hay,
And one black leather Bible with a broken spine.

I think of the bulls my father slaughtered every August,
How he would pull out of that rank sea
A pair of collapsed lungs, stomach,
Eight bushels of gleaming rope he called intestines,
And one bucket of parts he could never name.

In the dream that keeps circling back in the shape
Of a barn, my father has just drained
His last bull. Outside it is raining harder
Than I've ever seen, and the sky is about to step down
On one leg. And all through the barn,
As high as the loft, the smell of blood and hay.
All night, as long as the dream holds,
He keeps turning the thick slab of soap over and over,
Building the lather up like clouds in his hands.

Tornado

What was amazing was not
The damage so much, the barns
It buckled, the livestock it left dead.
Or the swath, a mile wide,
It carved through the cornfields,
Stalks sheared to the ground.
Or even the safe, the old Mosler
From the bank at Plainview,
We found days later half-
Buried in some back pasture.
But the sight of Gustafson,
Dazed but still alive, looking up
Like one of the just-born,
The newly blessed, his corncribs
Brimming over with coins,
His dry, drought-stricken fields
All green, lush with bills,
And no sound but the broken blades
Of the wind pump grinding lazily
To a halt, his hogs grunting
Into the sweet light of the saved.

Tornado

Wherever he was, he was holding
The dark brim of his hat.
He was thinking of the pole-sitters,
At sixty feet the shadows
Of their long poles
Reaching out in absurd proportions,
At sixty feet the whole county
As flat as a dance floor.
Outside shirts galloped on the lines,
The trees were breaking stride.
Far off a silo uncoiled
Into the clouds, a barn knelt,
A sow quietly rose from her sty.
Then the song on the radio died.
He thought of the ballroom
And the couples dancing
Around and around for days.
By then the drift of the sitters
Was so lovely he could see them all,
High on their stems, swaying
In long circles over the farmlands.
It was 1930, a Saturday, the whole sky
Was black with wreckage.
Wherever he was, was an entrance.
He was holding the dark brim
Of his hat as if tipping it.

Tornado

On Saturdays we chose Lyle catcher
for both sides. He was one
of the slow ones and was around
only to lob the balls back, or chase
our long flies into the graveyard
behind Our Lady of the Fields.
The day it came sweeping down,
long, dark, a root dropping low
as any crop duster, we were
under the pews, everyone but Lyle,
and could tell it touched close
by the way the long bell rope danced.
We were only nine, and hid there
until the calm came back,
until everything began to steam—
the fields, the gravestones,
the cracked trough of holy water—
even the fish Lyle was parading
around the infield, the fat gray carp
that had come swimming down
he said out of the clouds. Perhaps
it was the way he was breathing,
or how he held it up so we
could see the blood on its gills
that made us all believe
he had caught it over home plate,
right where he had lost so many in the sun.

Tornado

The last time we saw Gunderson's prize sow
She was rising over the floodlights
Of the poultry barns, pedaling off
Into a sky full of wreckage. If ever a sow
Was beautiful, it was she, 700 pounds
Of blue-ribbon pork rooted down
Deep in her wallow, her whole body lit
With gold chaff. The next morning
We found Gunderson rocking
In the middle of his pigsty,
Staring off toward the county line,
And all we could hear was the rain
And its thin ticking against the leaves,
The empty swill pail vibrating in his hands.

Tornado

I had seen Ferris wheels before,
But this one was tall as a silo.
And nights I could see it circling
Over Drabowski's barn, its gondolas
Rocking in the stars. That night
The tornado came sashaying
Over the farmlands, dragging up
Trees, dust, mile after mile
Of fence line, all you could hear
Were those long guy-wires
Vibrating through the rain,
A hum so deep farmers looked up
From their evening chores,
Women moved toward
Open windows expecting to find
The stars, and even outfielders
Forgot for a moment the words
Of the anthem, turned, and
With ball caps over their hearts,
Looked up at the long arc
Of the sky, could see it grinding
In the middle of Drabowski's field,
Its huge ghostly outline looming
Over the barns. And some
Small boy at the top, rocking
In the wreckage, his face
Through the rain looking down
From those intricate spokes of light.

At the Blessing of the Children in Lourdes, Winter Solstice

They never imagined it would be like this—
The gurneys suddenly slipping away,
The braces all unclasping like hands.
And then the wading out, arm in arm,
Into the waters, the ghostly flowering
Of the nightclothes. And for a moment
You can see them, out in the long columns
Of light, turning like white pinwheels,
The night so cold there's just their breath
Starting its long climb into the sky.
And scattered there in the smoke,
The crutches shining like wing bones,
The empty fleets of wheelchairs overturned,
Their wheels grinding on their starlit hubs.

Waiting for Trains at Col d'Aubisque

Four a.m. and rain since dark, rain dropping
From the slate roofs onto the stone walkway,
And all of us here—
The middle-aged mother and the child,
The three privates smoking
As only those going off
For good can smoke—
All of us standing at these windows,
Except the young boy out under the archway
Who has brought his father's coffin
Down out of these bare hills,
A small sheepherder's boy
Who doesn't care how old the night gets
Or how long this rain takes hold,
Only that his wool coat
Is folded neatly, and that his head rests
Over his father's shoulder,
For if this boy, this young dark-eyed Basque
From Col d'Aubisque
Whose skin will never again feel as wet
Or as wanted as it is
By all this rain,
If this small boy would talk
He would say we've stood here
At these windows for nothing,
And that when morning comes
And we step out into the cold light,
The words we've waited all night to say
We will have to turn into breath
And use to warm our hands.

At Betharram

Here a mile down at Betharram
The grottoes start winding
Through the earth.
The walls seep
With last year's rain,
And I go down, alone, breathing
An air that's never
Been breathed.
And the farther I go
The more I want it like this in the end—
The earth empty,
My lantern going out in the cold,
The stalactites burning
Like huge wet roots
In the dark.
There's a calm here at Betharram
Deeper than I have known,
And down this far
The heart slows and beats
As calmly as the water
That never stops,
That I hear
Far down in the caves
Dripping for miles through stone.

Sainte-Foy

In the Pyrenees they killed
Their animals with stones,
And before that
By running their herds
Into the blazing air of these foothills.
Here at the church of Sainte-Foy,
The blood of those animals
Comes back night after night.
It comes back as dust
On the old stonecutter,
The Béarnais I see
Walking at sundown
Up the long, rocky path.
It comes back as earth and stone,
As hard chunks of mortar
And clay I pull from the walls
And smell what is Sainte-Foy,
A silence so deep I could stay here
And breathe this cold forever,
All this dung and hay,
This wet uncut stone
That is Sainte-Foy—
A vow I take deep, and break
As my headlights go on,
And see in the graveyard out back,
Snout buried in mud and clay,
A hog big enough for slaughter,
A loose sow that grunts once
At my lights and doesn't move.
She stands there as I turn,
Her round pink back steaming
In the cold, feeding on the dead
And what the dead push up.

At the Olive Grove of the Resistance

He says that home is here,
Here where the earth falls apart
In our hands, and he points
To the one good eye they left him.
Half his world cut out, half
Buried here in the charred roots
Of his three olive trees, four fingers
Down where they made him go
On his knees, his face sliced
To the bone; left him to look up
And see his oxen riding a crown
Of blood into the hills, his trees
Burning, each olive blazing
Into light; left him to find his son
Facedown on the stone pathway,
His wife in the shed, her small
White breasts bruised; left him
To wander each night in the wind
Born in these black branches,
Or to stand in his small stone room
Spreading the olives like jewels
In the sink. And he tells me
The good ones go north
So he can pay for the luxury
Of this light, the one bare bulb
That's the only flower of his house.
And because I have come here
To listen, he cuts one open
And shows me its hard oily pit,
A small black stone wet
With light, drying in the wind
Born in his three olive trees.

The Generals at Sunrise

Think of them in the early mornings,
High up on their decks, standing watch
At the railings. LeMay, Westmoreland.

Think of them under the last stars,
Waiting for the first rooftops to flare,
Their ghostly breath rising over the lawns.

Think of them out there at that hour,
That cold ungodly hour before the dogs bark,
The trees wake, the birdbaths so quiet.

The Old Liberators

Of all the people in the mornings at the mall,
It's the old liberators I like best,
Those veterans of the Bulge, Anzio, or Monte Cassino
I see lost in Automotive or back in Home Repair,
Bored among the paints and power tools.
Or the *really* old ones, the ones who are going fast,
Who keep dozing off in the little orchards
Of shade under the distant skylights.
All around, from one bright rack to another,
Their wives stride big as generals,
Their handbags bulging like ripe fruit.
They are almost all gone now,
And with them they are taking the flak
And firestorms, the names of the old bombing runs.
Each day a little more of their memory goes out,
Darkens the way a house darkens,
Its rooms quietly filling with evening,
Until nothing but the wind lifts the lace curtains,
The wind bearing through the empty rooms
The rich far-off scent of gardens
Where just now, this morning,
Light is falling on the wild philodendrons.

Der Führer's Mercedes

The day it came barreling through,
      headed west on its tour
           of the heartland—

dark, sleek, and rocking
      high on a flatcar—
           all of us looking up

could feel the thunder,
      the air around us explode
           like the Reich.

You understand I was young,
      I knew nothing.
           Göring, Goebbels,

their names were years away.
      Still, all that day I carried it
           around inside me,

could feel it strain wildly
      at its ropes, the black
           canvas dragging

like a broken wing.
      All day I kept seeing
           its long thundering shadow

coming down hard,
      the dust and dead leaves
           it pulled into the morning air.

The *Hindenburg*

We were two days out in the cold
waters off Newfoundland,
hauling in the last of our lobster pots,
when we heard high up
the strange, unmistakable beating
of engines. And there, nosing down
out of the clouds, was
the *Hindenburg,* pride of the Nazis,
all crease and contour, so big
it was almost planetary.
And we stood back, marveling
at how beautiful it was, how buoyant,
shining like some bright summons
in the evening sky. Then
it dipped its great prow in salute
and sailed on, growing smaller
and smaller, until at last
it was gone, and left us there
with big swells, lightning,
black clouds massed at the horizon.

The Bombing of Dresden

It was the night
Of Fasching,
And those crossing
The Marienbrücke
Saw the cold drizzle
And black winter sky
Suddenly ignite
Into summer.
And for an hour
The pipes
In every cellar
Dripped and ran dry,
Glass doorknobs
Flowered into jewels,
And the grapes
Left out to smolder
On their vines
Burst into stones.
For an hour
The earth was a jar,
And every beet
And potato inside
Began to bleed.
The next morning
Those gathered
Along the Elbe
Saw the cold smoke
Of a blossom
And couldn't be sure
It was dawn,
That what they saw

Was the sun
Striking a fish
And the singed weaving
Of its gills.
And nothing was left
But the snails
Gripping the dry walls
Of the cisterns,
The snails
That overnight
Turned into limestone
To survive.

Where I Live

It's a big two-story, white clapboard farmhouse, pre–Civil War, with a sprawling wraparound veranda, two shady magnolias in front, a widow's walk on top. Out one window there's a beautiful view of a battlefield, a cemetery out another. No one remembers who won, or even what war it was, but the casualties must've been heavy. Graves Registry has been at it for years. All day they march back and forth from battlefield to cemetery, adding graves as they go. So many dead, so many shafts to fill. From the widow's walk you can see where they've turned the corn into crosses, whole fields of crosses, one bumper crop after another gleaming under the early morning sun.

The Snow Country

for Carolyn

Up on Verstovia the snow country is silent tonight.
I can see it from our window,
A white sea whose tide flattens over the darkness.
This is where the animals must go—
The old foxes, the bears too slow to catch
The fall run of salmon, even the salmon themselves—
All brought together in the snow country of Verstovia.
This must be where the ravens turn to geese,
The weasels to wolves, where the rabbits turn to owls.
I wonder if birds even nest on that floating sea,
What hunters have forgotten their trails and sunk out of sight.
I wonder if the snow country is green underneath,
If there are forests and paths
And cabins with wood-burning stoves.
Or does it move down silently gyrating forever,
Glistening with the bones of animals and trappers,
Eggs that are cold and turning to stones.
I wonder if I should turn, tap, and even wake you.

Herds

On clear nights when I walk
The path back home,
I see animals glistening with frost
High in the grasslands.

Legends say they are small
Seas of breath
Stranded from an age lit by snow,
That when thaw comes

They stray through the foothills,
Leaving a strange language
Free in the streams,
Herds of lichen grazing on stones.

Goddard Hot Springs

When you lie in these sweating streams
You are lying in the breath of your ancestors,
The old pioneers who sat here in these pools
Mapping trails to the mother lode.
You feel a fog drift through your body,
A voice that is strangely familiar
And still has stories to tell.

Photo: White Pass Trail, 1899

In this photo the upper third
Is so faded it looks like fog.
You can see a fine line of spruce
Leaning toward exposure,
A small wall of dirt with roots
Shooting through its bedrock.
The rest is a stockpile of mules
So bloated they could be cows.
Some remain only as haunches,
Some as ears swelled up like leaves.
And some are there full-blown
So you see every stalled ripple.
To the right where the fog drops off
Some are passing for boulders,
Some you could even stand on
And stare past the fog into a clearing,
And hear the miners working
Their way north, the echoes
Of stones piling up to stake a claim.

Ancestors

for Robert Davis

The Tlingit on this island tell a story about fog.
They say in its belly
The spirits of the drowned are turned into otters,
That on cold nights when the lowlands
Smolder with steam
The loon builds its nest in their voices.
And I remember you telling me
Of a clan of friends you had heard in a dream,
All quietly singing to themselves.
Ancestors, you said,
People you hadn't seen in years,
Each wrapped in otter
And offering a piece of last month's moon,
A small amulet that glittered
In the dark like bone.
And all around you could see baskets
Of berries glistening with rain
And deep in the fog fish sweetening on racks.

The Kelp-Cutters

Ten years since I buried
All the air I could,
And followed you
Down into the dark,
Your breath shimmering
Like stars on the kelp.
Joe, when we broke through
That last time and found
The boat gone, the air
So cold we lay there
Not saying a word,
Hand in hand, treading
Until your warm grip went slack—
Joe, I could do nothing
But ride with the kelp
Into dawn, rocking
In the cold slate,
Listening to myself pump
The damp night full of breath.

Great Bear

I always see him rolling
Slowly on his side,
Always drifting
Downwind with the moon—
A bank of soft darkness,
An old weathered dirigible
Floating low over the spruce
Toward the distant muskegs,
Where the milkweed
Burst like lights on a wet
Deserted airstrip.

Whiteout

Here on this ridge
The only color
Left is you,
And soon you too will fade.
The spruce have long
Returned to birch,
And the birch
Are quietly
Turning to snow.

Owls

Owls glide off the thin
Wrists of the night,
And using snow for their feathers
Drift down on either side
Of the wind.

I spot them
As I camp along the ridge,
Glistening over the streambeds,
Their eyes small rooms
Lit by stone lamps.

Why I Can't Sleep

Blame it on the juncos outside
The window, sopranos
In one tree, altos in another.
Not to mention the starlings
Blaring away on the wire,
And the bands of swallows
And flycatchers pelting the house
With their steady downpour
Of notes. And don't forget
The chickadees and those bawdy
Little tunes they're belting out
From the bushes, or the cardinals
Chortling away at the feeder
As the sun comes up.
I'm going to blame them all—
The larks, the buntings,
Even those bright little prodigies,
The finches, out there
As the great door of morning
Swings open, singing for all
Their worth on the fence posts,
Pouring their arias out in the maples.

This Morning I Could Do a Thousand Things

I could fix the leaky pipe
Under the sink, or wander over
And bother Jerry who's lost
In the bog of his crankcase.
I could drive the half mile down
To the local mall and browse
Through the bright stables
Of mowers, or maybe catch
The power-walkers puffing away
On their last laps. I could clean
The garage, weed the garden,
Or get out the shears and
Prune the rosebushes back.
Yes, a thousand things
This beautiful April morning. Or better yet I could just lie
Here in this old hammock,
Rocking like a lazy metronome,
And wait for the daylilies
To open. The sun is barely
Over the trees, and already
The sprinklers are out,
Raining their immaculate
Bands of light over the lawns.

Field Notes

The poet has only one tool, the voice, and it starts in silence.

✦

A good poem rises out of compelling need or vision, out of what Words-worth calls "a dedicated Spirit." Pry to the roots, the old familiar dark, to the sweet smell of peat and swamp water.

✦

Inspiration, the force that many believe drives the making of a poem, is usually what happens second, after much sitting and waiting, repeated drafting and recasting.

✦

Poetry is too generous, its capabilities too great and liberating, for it to be reduced to a simple tool of self-expression. When a poem loses touch with the outside world and becomes so cloistered it is meaningful to only a small coterie of people, it loses its vitality, range, and finally its mission.

✦

Poetry opens doors beyond the immediate and through the saving grace of the imagination rescues us from the deadening practicalities of our daily lives.

✦

A good poem breaks through the numbing, stultifying voice of our mass culture to successfully articulate, in all its breadth and meaning, a land-scape of conviction, a deeper circuitry that helps give life its necessary shape and substance.

✦

A good poem works toward the recovery of a fundamental ground, a place composed of shapes and contours, patterns and moments that are common to us all, a shared property where we are able to retrieve a certain communality of spirit.

◆

Perhaps more than any other human endeavor, poetry is capable of giving voice to the deepest yearnings of the spirit, and in so doing offers us insights into who we are, where we have come from, our values and aspirations.

◆

With its ability to transform individual experiences into spiritual acts, poetry creates a sacred language, one whose intent is to change life, as Rimbaud reminds us, not through embellishment but through consecration.

◆

Ultimately, it is not solely a question of being rooted in time and place, though these are important to any poet. In the end, the whole life of a poem depends on its being grounded spiritually.

◆

In the process of writing, the poet becomes caught up in the playful joys of discovery, of the imagination, in the immemorial spirit of the journey itself. Every poem is a gift, a grateful giving-back of what has been found on that journey.

◆

Prose is linear, poetry circular, a dance around the well. Like religion, it journeys toward communion, that place where all lines, spatial and spiritual, converge.

◆

Poetry is, in many ways, a sustained longing for home and reconciliation, the inseparability of subject and object, self and other.

＊

"Everywhere connections," Heraclitus writes, "combinations, fluid transitions." Every poem is a small creation myth, a healing song that reconstitutes the world at the moment of its conception, when all things were linked in natural unity.

＊

A good poem forges a compassionate pact with the world and, like all enduring pacts, it is one that in the end sustains and confirms—the poet's life, ours, and the great healing powers of language.

＊

When a poem is finished, there is a wonderfully rapturous moment when the poet is never more alive or the world more composed. For that brief moment, both the poet and the world come together in pride, possibility, and affirmation.

ACKNOWLEDGMENTS

I wish to thank the following publishers for permission to reprint poems and translations that previously appeared in *Snow Country* (Copper Canyon Press, 1975), *At the Home-Altar* (Copper Canyon Press, 1979), *County O* (Copper Canyon Press, 1984), *Tornadoes* (Ion Books, 1990), *Night Music: Poems of Rolf Jacobsen* (State Street Press, 1994), *The Old Liberators: New and Selected Poems and Translations* (Holy Cow Press, 1998), *The Bullfinch Rising from the Cherry Tree* (Brooding Heron Press, 2001), *The Roads Have Come to an End Now: Selected and Last Poems of Rolf Jacobsen* (Copper Canyon Press, 2001), *A Bumpy Ride to the Slaughterhouse: Prose Poems of Dag T. Straumsvåg* (Red Dragonfly Press, 2006), *The Dream We Carry: Selected and Last Poems of Olav H. Hauge* (Copper Canyon Press, 2008), *The Lure-Maker from Posio: Prose Poems of Dag T. Straumsvåg* (Red Dragonfly Press, 2011), *Poems Prose Poems* (Red Dragonfly Press, 2013), and *The Light under the Door* (Red Dragonfly Press, 2014).

Some of these poems and translations previously appeared in the following journals, to whose editors grateful acknowledgment is made: *Absinthe, Alaska Quarterly Review, The American Poetry Review, Arts & Letters, Askew, Beloit Poetry Journal, The Bloomsbury Review, Borealis, The Carolina Quarterly, Charitan Review, Chowder Review, Circumference, Colorado Review, Dacotah Territory, Epoch, 5 AM, The Fourth River, The Gettysburg Review, Great River Review, Greenfield Review, Hayden's Ferry Review, Ice Floe, International Poetry Review, Journal of Contemporary Anglo-Scandinavian Poetry* (UK), *Kansas Quarterly, Kenyon Review, Knockout, Literary Review, Luna, Mankato Poetry Review, Mead Magazine, Mid-American Review, The Midwest Quarterly, Midwest Review, Minnesota Monthly, The Missouri Review, Montana Review, The Nebraska Review, Nimrod, North Dakota Quarterly, Osiris, Paintbrush, Pembroke Magazine, Permafrost, Poetry, Poetry Daily, Poetry East, Poetry International, Poetry Ireland Review, Poetry Now, Poetry Review* (UK), *Poetry Wales, Porch, Portland Review, Puerto del Sol, Raccoon, Ruminator Review, Saint Ann's Review, Seattle Review, Solo Café, Solo Novo, Southern Poetry Review, Spillway, Three Rivers Poetry Journal, War Literature & the Arts, Water-Stone, West Branch,* and *Willow Springs.*

Grateful acknowledgment is also made to the Bush Foundation, McKnight Foundation, Minnesota State Arts Board, National Endowment for the Arts, North Carolina Arts Council, and Yaddo Foundation for their assistance, financial and otherwise, during the writing and translating of these poems.

I wish to express my deepest gratitude to Jim Hans, Lynne McMahon, Sherod Santos, Dag T. Straumsvåg, Michael Waters, and especially to my dear wife, Carolyn, for all their support and encouragement over the years. I also wish to thank Michael Wiegers, Joseph Bednarik, George Knotek, Tonaya Craft, and everyone at Copper Canyon Press for their unfailing commitment to making this book possible.

ABOUT ROBERT HEDIN

Born and raised in Red Wing, Minnesota, Robert Hedin is the author, translator, and editor of twenty-three volumes of poetry and prose. The recipient of many honors and awards for his work, including three National Endowment for the Arts Fellowships as well as fellowships from the Bush, McKnight, and Yaddo Foundations, he has taught at the University of Alaska, the University of Minnesota, St. Olaf College, and Wake Forest University. He is co-founder (with his wife, Carolyn) and former director of the Anderson Center, an artist retreat in Red Wing. His work has been featured on *The Writer's Almanac,* National Public Radio's *All Things Considered,* and in Ted Kooser's nationally syndicated column, American Life in Poetry. He lives in Frontenac, Minnesota.

INDEX OF TITLES

Poetry is vital to language and living. Since 1972, Copper Canyon Press has published extraordinary poetry from around the world to engage the imaginations and intellects of readers, writers, booksellers, librarians, teachers, students, and donors.

WE ARE GRATEFUL FOR THE MAJOR SUPPORT PROVIDED BY:

THE PAUL G. ALLEN
FAMILY FOUNDATION

CULTURE

golden
lasso

Anonymous
Jill Baker and Jeffrey Bishop
Donna and Matt Bellew
John Branch
Diana Broze
Sarah and Tim Cavanaugh
Janet and Les Cox
Catherine Eaton and David Skinner
Mimi Gardner Gates
Linda Gerrard and Walter Parsons
Gull Industries, Inc.
on behalf of William and Ruth True
The Trust of Warren A. Gummow
Elizabeth Hebert
Steven Myron Holl
Lakeside Industries, Inc.
on behalf of Jeanne Marie Lee

TO LEARN MORE ABOUT UNDERWRITING
COPPER CANYON PRESS TITLES,
PLEASE CALL 360-385-4925 EXT. 103

WE ARE GRATEFUL FOR THE MAJOR SUPPORT PROVIDED BY:

Maureen Lee and Mark Busto

Rhoady Lee and Alan Gartenhaus

Ellie Mathews and Carl Youngmann as The North Press

Anne O'Donnell and John Phillips

Suzie Rapp and Mark Hamilton

Joseph C. Roberts

Jill and Bill Ruckelshaus

Cynthia Lovelace Sears and Frank Buxton

Kim and Jeff Seely

Dan Waggoner

Austin Walters

Barbara and Charles Wright

The dedicated interns and faithful volunteers
of Copper Canyon Press

The Chinese character for poetry is made up of two parts: "word" and "temple." It also serves as pressmark for Copper Canyon Press.

This book is set in Reminga, a contemporary digital typeface by Xavier Dupré. Book design by VJB/Scribe.
Printed on archival-quality paper.